I AM by Michael

This book is for you

I hope it helps

I AM by Michael Tavon

Dear Reader

This is the first interactive book I have ever done. I hope this is something the not only engages but inspires you as well.

I'm eager to see your responses

Please tag @Bymichaeltavon on Instagram or @MichaelTavon on twitter/facebook so I can share your responses.

Objective 1) Finish the title so it can best describe you

Ex: I am <u>a Noodle head</u>

(Lame joke, don't use that lol)

Objective 2) fill in the blanks throughout the book and write the prompts I provided. I can't wait to see your responses

I AM by Michael Tavon

Hopeful

A broken heart is mendable

don't wallow in self-doubt.

Take the broken piece to recreate

Something stronger and richer. This

Time make it more exclusive, less
accessible. The heart needs to be

given to the people worthy of your
space.

Trying

You're putting in overtime effort
to make things work. The more you
pull the more they push you away.
You wish things would go back to
the way they were. Unfortunately,
the past is a flame you can't
rekindle. You may not see this now,
but redirecting your efforts into
your dreams will be more rewarding
than wasting time on a love that's
fizzled out.

Trying to Forget

I'm trying to forget the pain, but
the scars on my broken heart remind
me of the past everyday.

Confused

Where were you when I needed you?

Where were you when I longed for companionship?

Where were you when called I

you my friend?

Where were you when I was surrounded by my lonely thoughts?

Where were you when I wanted to celebrate my accomplishments?

Where were you when you said you loved me?

Take your time to answer this pop quiz. I know all the answers will

be the same, but I hope you prove
me wrong.

Tired

She is tired of giving

I AM by Michael Tavon

all her love to part-time lovers.

Constantly wasting time

trying to chase forever

in people who eventually disappear

Reminded.

She is reminded of the pain

caused by ghosts from the past

every night when she sleeps alone.

A Survivor

When life threw her stones

She made a mountain

When life blew storms her way

I AM by Michael Tavon

she made an ocean

No matter what obstacles

life presents

she finds a way to survive and
thrive

Affirmation I

I AM by Michael Tavon

I will take the time to heal
properly

I won't rush into new relationships

Because I hate being alone

I will learn to trust myself

I will learn to love my solitude

I will find the meaning behind my
suffering

I will overcome

Affirmation II

I am love

I am light

I am _____

The Moon

She was beautiful

I AM by Michael Tavon

Like the night

I gazed into her eyes

They shined brighter than the moon

In that moment I knew

She was the one my soul

Craved for

The Sun

Her passion is more intense

Than the sun in July

I AM by Michael Tavon

Sparks fly when she smiles

Hearts melt when they stare

Her energy radiates

From afar

She has the power

To shed light in any space.

The Ocean

She is as peaceful as ocean waves

She brings out the beauty on rainy
days

Monsters

I AM by Michael Tavon

Monsters may come in the form of
smiles and empty promises. They say
anything that will lure hopeful
hearts into their domain. They take
advantage of innocent lovers
because of the heartache they
endured from past lovers

I forced my heart to fall in love
with the idea of some people, in

hopes of filling the void of
loneliness.

Too patient

I AM by Michael Tavon

She waited for a man who was ready
for love

But wasn't ready to love her

Obsession

Sometimes, that person might not be
infatuated with you, they just like
the idea of you wanting them.

Self.

The voyage to self-discovery gets
turbulent at times. The waves, the
motion, the unknown, gets scary.
The longer you travel the more
challenging it gets, that's what
it's all about. Facing your
hardships will lead you to the
fruitful destination you are
fighting to reach.

Fighting

She is fighting to be understood by
people who counted her out.
Climbing from the bottom to get
noticed by people who don't care. I
hope, by the time she reaches the
top; she will no longer feel the
need to be validated by irrelevant
people.

Wanting.

I AM by Michael Tavon

You ever wanted someone so bad

But the timing wasn't right

you spend lonely days

And lonely ass night with
thoughts

Of them on your mind

It's 3:35 in the am

And I can sleep

Because of her

If you're listening

I wish you were here.

<u>Solitude</u>

I AM by Michael Tavon

I wish I could live
Alone on the moon
So I can feel real freedom
Free from pain
free from lies
Free from money
Free from warfare
Free from death
Free from all negativity

All I would need is
Food and Wifi
I would be just fine
Alone on the moon
With my love and music

Amazing

Her pussy has the power to turn
a stray man faithful.

Understanding

Never lose your sanity over someone
who hurts you without a care

Affirmation III

I am in love with my refection

I am infatuated with my soul

I am pleased with my growth

I am thankful for growing old

Affirmation IV

It hurts now, but the pain will
shape me into best version of
myself.

Affirmation V

I AM by Michael Tavon

All storms are temporary

This too shall past

Consent II

I AM by Michael Tavon

There are too many classes teaching
daughters how to defend themselves
Against predators, but no classes
teaching sons how to treat women.
The concept of consent is so
foreign to too many men, and I
wonder where did the parents go
wrong? Why do so many men feel
entitled to bodies that don't
belong to them? Why do they feel
the need to pressure women to get
what they want? Why do they feel so
comfortable with disrespecting
women? Where did the parents go
wrong?

Crying

I wish I never cried over you.

Tug of War

You should never play tug of war
with your peace. Some people only
come into your life to disrupt your
bliss. Your peace is not a game and
when someone decides to tug and
pull, let go of the rope and watch
them fall as your peace remains
intact.

Generous

She's emotionally wealthy,

I AM by Michael Tavon

And generous when it comes to

giving to those who need it

Even when people come and go,

take advantage of her heart

It doesn't stop her

she refuses to become selfish

when it comes to giving

because she doesn't want to

shortchange the people in despair

Gotta Love Her

I AM by Michael Tavon

Gotta love a woman

who is fearless

In her expression

Confident with her intellect

And proud of her sexuality

I AM by Michael Tavon

A Miracle

She prays to god for a miracle

Without realizing she is one

Compromising

I AM by Michael Tavon

Sometimes, a compromise is

necessary to improve the quality of

a relationship, but never

compromise so much to the point you

become a shell of yourself

Affirmation VI

Today, will be a win

I owe it to myself

To win.

Brother to Brother

I'm not here to bash men

I AM by Michael Tavon

Or belittle them for some the
mistakes some have made

I'm far from perfect

But over time I became

Accountable for my own bullshit

I am here to help my brothers

Grow, I want them to learn from
their mistakes too

In plain sight

Heartbreak is bitch from hell,

I AM by Michael Tavon

but don't let it turn you into a
vindictive person.

Through the pain

You must handle it with grace

Take a step back

Rest

Reset

Heal in plain sight

Phenomenal

Sex with her is phenomenal

But the conversations after

Drives my mind wild.

An Explorer

A woman who isn't afraid to explore
in bed is a woman worth traveling
with.

A Poet

She doesn't need whiskey to speak
her truth; all she need is a pen
and solitude

Heal First

Heal before you search for love
Again, using relationships as a
coping mechanism is not healthy,
it's self- destructive

A Love Theory

I AM by Michael Tavon

Some people like to believe they
can change, but the people who hurt
them can't. that's a selfish way to
think. In my opinion, everyone
deserves a chance to learn and grow
from the pain they caused. Everyone
who hurts you isn't a bad person,
maybe they weren't mature enough or
ready for commitment. Some are in
love with the idea of love, but not
ready to put in the work. If you
can grow from your mistakes, they
can too.

I AM by Michael Tavon

Affirmation VII:

I am in the process of

_____

_____

I am aware of the work it will take

I am ready for the challenge.

Affirmation VIII:

Today, my heart is filled with joy

And I will spread as much a love

into the atmosphere as possible

Affirmation IX:

I believe I have what it takes to

_____

And I will not allow anything to

hold me back, not even myself.

I AM by Michael Tavon

Ambition

Her drive attracts attention

From people who want to join the
ride

if you aren't willing to add fuel

to her engine

don't interrupt her journey

watch her travel

and admire her ambition

Dark Thoughts

To the people who doubt themselves
into an anxiety attack

To the people who overthink
themselves into depression

It's easy to allow those dark
thoughts to consume you

Please, relax

Stop abusing yourself

You're not a failure

You're not falling behind

Just because things aren't
happening when you want them to

Doesn't mean

your dreams won't come true

Fake Belief

We seem to fall for liars

And question the real ones.

Why?

I AM by Michael Tavon

Maybe, because liars tell us what

we want to hear, to make us feel

good, so they can get what they

want.

While the honest people

Say what we truly feel

But afraid to accept

The truth hurts

And lies brings fake bliss

The Truth about Magic

I AM by Michael Tavon

Lies are like magic tricks,

They create illusions to the

heart and eyes,

tangible enough for gullible

minds to believe

and mysterious enough

to keep people intrigued

I AM by Michael Tavon

Life without love just feels empty

Prompt # 1

I AM by Michael Tavon

Write a note to the younger you:

I AM by Michael Tavon

Prompt #2

I AM by Michael Tavon

Write a note to the future you:

Prompt #3

Write a note to your first
heartbreak thanking them for the
lesson they taught you.

I AM by Michael Tavon

I AM by Michael Tavon

Petals

I AM by Michael Tavon

Some roses remain torn after
storms, others grow back with
stronger petals.

I AM by Michael Tavon

When your mind craves for
substance, stop feeding it basic
shit.

Affirmation X

I am unlearning

My past idea of love

Because it's hindering my ability

To grow and think freely.

Affirmation XI

I am not defined by the error of my
past ways, I am moving forward with
what I have learned, so I won't
repeat the same habits over and
over again.

The Standard

She wants what she can't have
because they are not ready to live
up to her standards.

Printed in Poland
by Amazon Fulfillment
Poland Sp. z o.o., Wrocław